THE LOST GOSPEL OF THOMAS

The Original Mystical Teachings of Yeshua

Collected and Edited

by

Theodore J. Nottingham

ISBN 9780985907457
Printed in the United States of America.

Table of Contents

Foreword

By Theodore J. Nottingham

The oral tradition of passing wisdom on from Teacher to student is the most ancient way of the transmission of transformational knowledge. Beyond doctrines, human-made creeds, institutions, and cultural accretions, exists the living and life-giving consciousness of the Master who breathes words into the souls of receptive seekers of the Sacred. These words have surfaced after two thousand years to speak to an age where the unity of humanity has become more evident than ever before. Spiritual teachings from the remotest parts of the world have entered the western world, including the forgotten wisdom of early eastern Christianity. It is for this time in human history that the Gospel of Thomas has been preserved and rediscovered against all odds.

The potent spiritual instructions and intuitive insights transcending space-time offer us nothing less than a rebirth of the original revelations of the long awaited Anointed One whose teachings have been distorted, perverted and turned into their opposite by human ignorance and mercilessness from the first century onward. We have the opportunity in our time to breathe the same mystic consciousness as the first disciples, as Yeshua the Nazarene Himself, just as Christianity disintegrates into a hopeless apostasy of itself. This is how important these words are. They can save the eternal and universal Truth originally brought into humanity for the purpose of creating a new humanity. At the eleventh hour, the spiritual core of the Way has been placed before us again before it is too late.

Each individual must face this cosmic opportunity for themselves. Each one must choose the "road less traveled" and accept that the Son of Man still has no place to lay His head in this world.

That "road less traveled by" is a modern parallel to the ancient mystical metaphor *"the way is narrow that leads to life, and there are few who find it"* (Matthew 7:14) This less traveled, more difficult "road" is the living out of a spiritual life rather than a mere survival in our short passage through time. In exploring the inner meaning of spiritual teachings, it is necessary to go beyond the standard dogmas that are passed on through catechism, Sunday-school classes and theological seminaries. From the very beginning, there was an inner understanding of the teachings that had to be uncovered. Jesus said to his disciples: *"To you has been given the secret of the kingdom of God, but for those outside everything is in parables."* (Mark 4:11) Contemporary theologians are very uncomfortable with this and they try to dismiss it along with other sayings such as "the Kingdom of God is within you" which is consistently translated "among you" because they cannot accept the implications of that little Greek preposition *en.*

One thing is certain: any search for transforming Truth, the kind that opens the inner sight to a radically new sense of reality, cannot be undertaken on the surface of our secular, materialistic society. That plane is made up exclusively of the search for food, mates, and success. It is the world of the absurd and the tragic, where people seem to be born in order to pay the rent, produce more consumers and workers for the anthill, and then die when their value as laborers is over. In such a life, there is no mystery, no wonder, no higher purpose, no hope.

Those who intuitively recognize that this cannot possibly be the sum total of the purpose for existence must find their way into deeper undercurrents of civilization where another kind of knowledge is available to humanity, beyond the "eat or be eaten" syndrome. In other words, they must come upon "the road less traveled." Unfortunately, these subterranean levels include all sorts of quicksands and obstacles, and one must be prepared to struggle with dangerous traps in order to reach higher planes of understanding.

This blind hunger for experience of a wiser, vaster

plane of reality comes from a deep inner yearning. It is particularly prevalent now that the worldview of the dominant cultures excludes this reality. Quite often, this need for experience of the transcendent is distorted into a return to the ancient world of omens and amulets, which seems more interesting than the world of shopping malls and fast food restaurants.

The ancient Scriptures that are the foundation of Christianity invite us to seek after the mystery and power that we name God, but whose Name is too sacred to speak. They tell us that this unknown and yet very present Creative Force of the universe responds to us individually. But they add that a personal contact must be established to enable our participation in this new consciousness, that is, in order to walk the less traveled path into the "undiscovered country" of spirit.

The experience of encounter yields with the Divine generates a transformation, an awakening which opens onto another dimension of reality known in the symbolism of religious language as *life eternal*. *"And this is eternal life, that they <u>know</u> the only true God..." (John 17:3).*

This highest state of consciousness whch the Apostle Paul described as "the peace that passes all understanding" (I like the translation – *"that no one understands"*) has been given many names.

At the turn of the century, Rudolf Otto named it *"the Mysterium Tremendum"* and R.M. Bucke called it *"cosmic consciousness."* Zen Buddhism names it *Satori*, in Yoga it is *Samadhi*, in Taoism they know it as *"the absolute Tao."* In our day, Thomas Merton used the phrase *"transcendental unconscious"* while Abraham Maslow describes it as *"peak experience"*; the Sufis speak of *Fana* and G.I. Gurdjieff labeled it *"objective consciousness"* while the Quakers experience it as *"the Inner Light."* Karlfried Graf Dürckheim

calls it the *"breakthrough of Being."*

What is meant by these mysterious expressions of the

experience of enlightenment, illumination, liberation,

mystical oneness? At its most basic level, we are dealing

with a state of awareness that is radically different from our

ordinary understanding. The word *mysticism*, so abused and

rejected in mainstream religious circles, simply suggests an

expansion of consciousness beyond the ordinary

boundaries of our egos to a state where union with a

greater reality is achievable. Evelyn Underhill defines

mysticism as "the hunger for reality, the unwillingness to be

satisfied with the purely animal or the purely social level of

consciousness." This is the first and essential stage in the

development of a mystical consciousness.

The less traveled road, or the mystic way as others

might call it, is therefore a process of sublimation carrying the relationship of the self with the universe to higher levels than our ordinary states of awareness. But this is no selfish journey. For as the mystic grows nearer the source of true life and participates in the creative energies of the Divine, he or she is capable of greater unselfish activity to the point of unconditional Love.

We learn from the writings of the mystics that such a consciousness has the power to lift those who possess it to a plane of reality that no struggle, no cruelty, no catastrophe can disturb. This "inner sanctuary" is the point where God and the soul touch. In the fourteenth century, John Tauler referred to this place as "the ground of the soul." Catherine of Siena spoke of the "interior home of the heart," Teresa of Avila knew it as the "inner castle," and John of the Cross described it as the "house at rest in darkness and concealment." These metaphors suggest a secret dwelling in the center of our being that remains permanently united with God's creative act. The self in its deepest nature is more than itself. To move into oneself means ultimately to move beyond oneself. But this does not wrap us in a selfish isolation from the pain and responsibility of life. Rather, it renews and empowers us to reach out to others in truly meaningful ways. Evelyn Underhill tells us that such inner transformation helps the mystics to enter, more completely than ever before, into the life of the group to which they belong:

> It *will teach them to see the world in a truer proportion, discerning eternal beauty beyond and beneath apparent ruthlessness. It will educate them in a charity free from all taint of sentimentalism; it will confer on them an unconquerable hope.*

Out of her vast study and personal experience, Underhill offers us one of the finest definitions of *mysticism*: "Mysticism is the way of union with Reality. The mystic is a person who has attained that union in greater or lesser degree; or who aims at and believes in such attainment."

Throughout Western history, most religious or spiritual teachings have emphasized the goal of human life and underplayed or neglected *the means by which this goal may be reached.* This is the journey of the one who chooses "the road less traveled" and there are many who have witnessed to the fact that this harder road, this narrow way, is an inner journey leading to the infinite depths of our True Self, crossing the threshold into becoming a conscious Child of God, a Child of the Universe. This the goal and purpose of the "secret" or "inner" teachings of Yeshua re-discovered in our time in their pristine and original form.

Introduction

The well-known professor Elaine Pagels offers us a succinct and laser-sharp insight into the purpose and meaning of the Gospel of Thomas:

In this gospel, and this is also the case in the Gospel of Luke, the Kingdom of God is not an event that's going to be catastrophically shattering the world as we know it and ushering in a new millennium. Here, as in Luke 17:20, the Kingdom of God is said to be an interior state; "It's within you," Luke says. And here it says, "It's inside you but it's also outside of you." It's like a state of consciousness. It's

hard to describe. But the Kingdom of God here is

something that you can enter when you attain gnosis,

which means knowledge. But it doesn't mean intellectual

knowledge. The Greeks had two words for knowledge.

One is intellectual knowledge, like the knowledge of

physics or something like that. But this gnosis is personal,

like "I know that person, or do you know so and so." So

this gnosis is self-knowledge; you could call it insight. It's a

question of knowing who you really are, not at the ordinary

level of your name and your social class or your position.

But knowing yourself at a deep level. The secret of gnosis is

that when you know yourself at that level you will also

come to know God, because you will discover that the

divine is within you.

Now, in the Gospel of Thomas, this Jesus comes to reveal that you and he are, if you like, twins.... And what you discover as you read the Gospel of Thomas, which you're meant to discover, is that you and Jesus at a deep level are identical twins. And that you discover that you are the child of God just as he is. And so that at the end of the gospel Jesus speaks to Thomas and says, "Whoever drinks from my mouth will become as I am, and I will become that person, and the mysteries will be revealed to him." Here, Jesus does not take the role of authority and teacher. In the Gospel of Thomas, the disciples say to Jesus, "Tell us, what do you want us to do? How shall we pray? What shall we eat? How shall we fast?" Now if you look at Matthew and Luke, Jesus answers the questions. He says, "When you pray, say, 'Our Father who are in Heaven, hallowed be...' When you fast, wash your face, don't make a show of it. When you give alms do it privately and without being

19

showy." In this gospel, this Jesus does not answer. He says, "Do not tell lies, and do not do what you hate, for everything is known before heaven." Now this answer throws you and me upon ourselves.... Here Jesus, in effect, turns one toward oneself, and that is really one of the themes of the Gospel of Thomas, that you must go in a sort of a spiritual quest of your own to discover who you are, and to discover really that you are the child of God just like Jesus.

1

The Discovery

Matthew Thomas Farrell shares a stricking exposition of how the lost Gospel was found:

One morning, Muhammad 'Ali al-Samman and his brother Khalifah saddled up their camels and rode off for the Djebel el-Tarif, a near-by mountain. The journey would take them several hours, so during the trip they talked. Mostly, their discussions focused on a man who lived in a near-by village. His name was Ahmad Hawara.

The two brothers were plotting his murder.

Back in May, Ahmad had killed Muhammad 'Ali's father, the latest victim of an ongoing blood feud. Muhammad 'Ali wished to avenge his dad's death, and bandied ideas with Khalifah on how best to achieve this ghoulish goal. At his side he had a mattock, which his mother advised him to keep sharp, should they happen to find the monster who made her a widow. For now, however, he intended to use it to dig sabakh, a soft nitrogen-rich soil that is good natural fertilizer.

They reached Djebel el-Tarif, an imposing mound with over one hundred and fifty caves, and chose a suitable place to hobble their camels. Muhammad 'Ali began to dig around a boulder, and to his surprise encountered something solid buried in the ground. Quickly, he unearthed a large clay pot, caked with ages of earth. The top, he saw, was sealed on with bitumen.

Muhammad 'Ali pondered this a moment, extremely uneasy. After all, just to the north on another side of el-Tarif was an old graveyard. Officials who served the pharaohs of the Sixth Dynasty with distinction were interned there. He considered the jar before him, mattock in hand. To him, there was the very real possibility that it might contain a djinn, and breaking it open would release it. Muhammad 'Ali had no desire to free (and then confront) an evil spirit. But of course, it might also contain gold. He weighed his options, and greed conquered superstition. Hefting his mattock, he smashed open the top.

A shower of tiny golden flakes rose up on crests of stale air, to be carried away by the wind. Leaning over, Muhammad

'Ali looked inside. He found it held, not gold or spirits, but thirteen leather-bound books, filled with crumbling, yellowed pages that flaked off and blew away as he pulled the tomes out to examine them. The pages were cracked and brittle, and filled with an elegant calligraphy totally lost on his illiteracy.

He had no idea what they were, but was certain of one thing: these books were ancient.

Which meant that they were valuable. Antiques dealers in Cairo just loved these things, and paid good money for them. So, wrapping them in his tunic, he returned home and put them on a bed of straw right next to the stove. His mother was pleased: not only had her son brought fertilizer for their crops, he apparently found some kindling as well.

Her joy became even greater a month later when she learned that Ahmad was nearby. She urged her sons to go seek vengeance, and then tossed another codex on the fire to brew up a cup of tea. Muhammad 'Ali and his six brothers carried out their mission with a zeal that would have made mama proud. In fact, they attacked Ahmad while he was asleep, and "...hacked off his limbs bit by bit, ripped out his heart, and devoured it among them, as the ultimate act of blood revenge."[1]

Unfortunately for them, the person they had chosen to kill was the son of the local sheriff. Ahmad was not very popular, and the villagers (who had eagerly shown Muhammad 'Ali where Ahmad was) suddenly suffered acute amnesia regarding the whole affair. During the investigation, Muhammad 'Ali learned that the authorities were going to search his house for evidence. He decided it prudent to sequester the books, until he could eventually get to Cairo to sell them. He gave several to friends for safe-keeping. He also gave one to a Coptic priest, knowing that a priest's house would hardly be searched. The priest agreed to keep it for him, and put it aside without looking at it.

Coptic priests can marry, and this priest's brother-in-law happened to be visiting. He saw Muhammad 'Ali's codex, suspected its value, and promptly stole it. He took it to an antiques dealer in Cairo, who bought it for 250. Most, if not all, of Muhammad 'Ali's "friends" did likewise over the next year as the homicide investigation dragged on. This eventually attracted the attention of the Department of Antiques, who began to acquire them (and ultimately resorted to nationalization to get possession.)

Still, several of the codices made a successful exodus from Egypt. One was purchased by the Carl Jung Foundation and presented to the psychologist on his ightieth birthday. The CJF made the first serious attempt to translate their work, which turned out to be an anthology containing titles such as The Prayer of the Apostle Paul, The Apocryphon (i.e.: "Secret Book") of James, The Gospel of Truth, and The Treatise on the Resurrection. Unfortunately, numerous pages were missing, making any sort of translation at that point difficult at best.

In an effort to solve this, Professor Giles Quispel investigated the history of the codex and flew to the Coptic Museum in Cairo where the surviving texts had eventually been acquired. It turned out that they did have most of the missing pages from what is now known as the Jung Codex, and they agreed to give him photographs of the missing pages, plus several of the other texts as well. Hurrying back to his hotel room, Quispel began deciphering the ancient manuscripts.

His curiosity quickly turned to astonishment when the very first thing he read was:

These are the secret words which the living Jesus spoke, and which the twin, Judas Thomas, wrote down.

After nearly two millennia, The Gospel According to Thomas had finally been found.

2

The Presentation of Key Passages

With materials made available from Jean-Yves Leloup and Tau Malachi

Among all the astonishing documents accidentally—or fatefully—unearthed in 1945 near the desert village of Nag Hammadi in Upper Egypt, the Gospel of Thomas has made the greatest impact on our understanding of Christianity. The first English rendering of this text was published in 1959 and was greeted with intense interest by scholars and theologians alike. But the impact of this document was soon felt far beyond the circles of specialists, almost as though an audible recording of the voice of Jesus had been discovered. Even across the reaches of millennial time and even through the veil of translation from languages known to but a few, for many of us the words in this text have the power to touch an unknown part of ourselves that brings with it an undeniable recognition of truth and hope.

When it was said of Jesus, by those who were at first bewildered by him, that he spoke "as one having authority," what is surely meant is that he and his teaching authenticated itself by their power to awaken that same hidden, self-authenticating part of the human heart and mind.

"It is my belief," Jean-Yves Leloup writes, "that it is from this ground [of inner silence], rather than from mental agitation, that these words [of Yeshua] can bear their fruit of light."

"Is it possible," Leloup asks, "to read these logia [these sayings of Yeshua] in a way that allows them to make their way into the mind and the heart of our humanity, leading us into a voyage of transformation, toward a full realization of our being?" Within this question lie both the effort and the reward, the demand and the gift, offered by this and all truly sacred writings.

The Gospel of Thomas was missing for almost two millennia until three copies of it were almost miraculously discovered several decades ago: two sections of it written in Greek found in Egypt, and a more complete edition in the Coptic language found near Nag Hammadi buried under the sands of time in a clay storage jar. Practically predicting itS own rediscovery, the Book of Thomas says: "Know what is before your face, and what is hidden from you will be revealed to you. For there is nothing hidden which will not be revealed, nor anything buried which will not be raised." (Saying Five)

While we imagine ourselves to be the most technologically advanced and enlightened society that has ever existed, we remain blind to the chains that shackle modern people which can be portrayed in the reality of a simple Gospel proclamation in the words: "(3) Jesus said ...But if you will not know yourselves, you dwell in poverty and it is you who are that poverty".

This is a contemplative "wisdom gospel," with its format of proverbs and parables. It contains absolutely no narrative whatsoever. It's comprised solely of one hundred and fourteen unvarnished sayings of Jesus, one after the other, and that's it. There is no commentary, and no story. No more Roman centurions, scribes, Pharisees, and locusts to block our view. Rather than being presented through the "lens" of others, the reader encounters a more direct, unfiltered historic Jesus. The intention by those who compiled and circulated this collection is to encourage readers to deeply ponder each and every saying for themselves, leading them to their own personal insights and revelations, to internalize the words and be transformed by them.

Though nowadays associated with Egypt, these surviving pages are copies of an even earlier Greek manuscript most likely originating from Syria, which was, and remains, home-base of the "Saint Thomas Branch of Christianity," the Syriac-Aramaic Church of the East. It is said that Saint

Thomas during the First Century AD headed east,

eventually ending up in India, where he spent the rest of his

life.

The Living Master said to his initiates: "What your own

eyes cannot see, your human ears do not hear, your

physical hands cannot touch, and what is inconceivable to

the human mind – that I will give to you!" (Saying

Seventeen).

The Master taught his disciples that in order to see the

spiritual realm, they must "fast from the world" and enter

into heavenly repose (Sabbath rest) – rise above mental

impressions, memories, worries, and agitations. They must

set aside some time to rest spiritually, to temporarily close

their physical eyes (and ears) to the outside world in order to "see the Father", the Supreme Being, with the eye of the soul. (Saying Twenty-Seven)

The Egyptian mystic Evagrius wrote: "The offspring of pure prayer is swallowed up by the Spirit. From this point on, the mind is beyond prayer, and prayer has ceased from it now that it has found something even more excellent. No longer does the mind actually pray, but there is a gaze of wonder at the Inaccessible Things which do not belong to the world of mortal beings."

"We have come from the Light." (from Gospel of Thomas, Saying Fifty-One) "For you have come from it, and you will return there again." (from Saying Forty-Nine)

So a living teacher by the name of Yeshua once taught his living students that they would be able to experience "entering the Kingdom," the other dimensions of Inner Space at the heart of the Present by seeing Divine Light. "If your eye be Single, your whole body will be full of Light." (Saying preserved in Matthew 6:22) "For this reason I say, if one is whole, one will be filled with Light, but if one is divided, one will be filled with darkness." (Yeshua, from Saying Sixty-One).

Becoming "a Single One," a spiritually whole person united with God, was the goal of the Thomas tradition of Syrian mysticism. "When you make the two into one... then you will enter the Kingdom." (Saying Twenty-Two) The spirit, mind and body of the mystic all become united in God; its new way of being is "Singleness." The word for "Single One" or "Singleness" in the Syriac-Aramaic language is "Ihidaya," and is used to describe souls that enter into mystical oneness. The hermits of the Syrian tradition eventually were called "the Ihidaya." However, "Ihidaya" isn't merely a title, office, or a robe that one puts on, but is a matter of spiritual realization, an interior state of being, an individual experience, a mystical level of awareness that is reached by a contemplative soul.

"There is Light within a Person of Light, and it illuminates the entire cosmos." (Saying Twenty-Four).

But although the texts themselves can now be directly seen for the first time in nearly two thousand years, to really see them is a task that invites us to something much more demanding and joyous than simply reading them according to familiar habits of intellectual analysis. It is not for nothing that in this document the very first words of Jesus, here called by the Aramaic name Yeshua, are these: "Whoever lives the interpretation of these words will no longer taste death." Is there some kind of knowing that can transform our being to the point—dare we imagine—of bringing forth a life that does not die when the body dies?

This Gospel of Thomas contains no biography of Jesus, nor any account of his miracles. It is a collection of 114 sayings, called logia in Greek (singular: logion). These are said to be the naked words attributed to the Master, "the Living Jesus," written down by Didymus Judas Thomas, the Twin.

What interests Thomas is the transmission of Yeshua's teaching. Every saying received from the Master is treated as a seed, with the potential of growing a new kind of fully conscious human being.

While we may look to see the depth of Wisdom contained in a verse, and gain an understanding of various levels of meaning intended, we can also seek what the verse draws out from the depths of our own being—— an expression of our holy soul or Divine self . Jesus said, "He who drinks from my mouth will become like me. I myself will become he, and the things that are hidden will be revealed" (Gospel of St. Thomas , Verse 108). To "drink" from the mouth of the Master and to become like him is to draw out the various teachings to be found in the different layers of meaning in the Scriptures, the Master becoming the person who is drawing forth the Wisdom of one's own holy soul and Christ-self. Only in this way are "the things that are hidden" revealed. This process of seeking knowledge, understanding, and wisdom must be more than merely the formation of mental concepts.

LOGION 1

Whoever lives the interpretation of these words will no longer taste death.

The Living Yeshua is speaking in secret, within, behind your heart. Christ dwells there within you, and when you go within, Christ will speak the secret teachings to you and lead you in the path of awakening. To listen and hear, *you must be silent.* You must *empty yourself of yourself* and let the Christ-Spirit fill you. Dying to yourself, you must *be conceived and reborn* of the Holy Spirit as the Living Yeshua. Indeed, as Jean-Yves Leloup states so profoundly, you must "experience the same conception, gestation, and birth as the Living Yeshua so that you also might be his twin, born of the same birth from the Holy Virgin, Mother Wisdom."

Everyone is the Living Yeshua. The ordinary person is ignorant of this, but the apostle of God knows it and lives according to the Truth and Light *revealed through experience.* Likewise, the kingdom of heaven is here and now, within you and all around you. It is present within everyone. The ordinary person does not have eyes to see it, but the one who knows perceives it and so dwells in the kingdom of God *here and now.*

Logos (Word) and Sophia (Wisdom) are to be found within everyone and everything, and so also within you. There, within your secret center, at the core of your being, is the Holy One. The Christ-Self is your true self, the Self of every self and soul of every soul. All are united with him in the Sacred Unity that is God. The Holy Spirit indwells the whole of Creation. Knowing this, you will not experience death.

Written or spoken, the secret remains a secret *until it is part of your own experience.* The teachings are received only when they are your own experience. Then they become *a living initiation*— a Light-transmission.

Some would translate "apocryphal words" in the literal sense of the Greek word apokruphos, which simply means "hidden." But this prologue implies much more that: Yeshua has come to reveal to us the Words of the Secret, of the Human and of the Divine: God in Human and Human in God . . . the secret of Being and of Love.

The God of Love who dwells in the depths of human beingness is a secret, and it is from these hidden depths that we can act, think, and speak in true freedom. Yeshua, the Living, the Awakened One, reveals through his words, his life, and his acts the secret that all human beings *can realize and manifest.* He fully incarnates life and love, which is why he is given the name the Living One, the *revealer of that which we can attain if we allow ourselves to be and live in the Presence of God.*

What will death mean to that one who experiences Messianic consciousness and dwells in the kingdom of God while in this life? Indeed, death will not mean what it means to the ordinary person, for that one is not so self-identified with mortal name and form, but knows oneself as an immortal Spirit, a bornless and therefore deathless Spirit. Likewise, this person knows that the kingdom of heaven is present within and all around, always— that upon death one's experience of Christ will continue in a more subtle and sublime form, having shed the physical body. With this knowledge, death is no longer death and the adversary has no power over the soul, whether in this world or in the world to come. Such a person is awakened and therefore free, having a continuity of awareness throughout all states of existence . Death will come, as it has for all prophets and saints, but it will just be an appearance of departure— a transition to another mode of existence, no more or less real than falling asleep, only to dream and awaken again. Death, for the Gnostic, is not an end as much as a new beginning. Ultimately, death has no substantial reality, but is merely a natural moment of transition. Knowing this changes everything.

LOGION 2

Yeshua said: Whoever searches must continue to search until they find. When they find, they will be disturbed; and being disturbed, they will marvel and will reign over All.

This logion describes the major stages in gnosis, which constitute a true initiatory process. The first stage is the quest; the second is the discovery; the third is the shock and disturbance of this discovery; the fourth is wonder and amazement; and the fifth is the presence and reign over All.

In the fourth century C.E., Gregory of Nyssa said: "Concepts create idols of God of whom only wonder can tell us anything." The Greek philosophical tradition also saw wonder and astonishment as the beginning of wisdom. In our own time, Einstein remarked that only idiots are incapable of wonder—and we might define idiots as those who forsake their quest, thinking that they know. The more we discover, the more we marvel and wonder. But these two are not some kind of romantic imagination or fantasy. For Einstein, wonder lay in the fact that at certain moments the world becomes intelligible, that there is a possibility of resonance between our intelligence and the Cosmos, as if they were both animated by the same consciousness. Only after experiencing this wonder can we enter into the mystery of that which reigns over All.

This seeking is the sacred quest for the Holy Grail, which is not a physical relic or holy cup outside of oneself. Rather, the Holy Grail is a purified and consecrated heart, soul, mind, and life; it is oneself open and sensitive to the Christ-Spirit so that one lives the life of Christ . The Grail is the heart in which the Lord dwells , the person who has discovered an innate Spirit-connection and who lives within.

When seeking is based upon preconception, precondition, and expectations, upon who and what you think you are and who and what you believe reality or God to be , then seeking itself becomes an obstruction and what is sought cannot be discovered. If you go looking for something that does not exist or go seeking in a way or in a place it cannot be found, then, indeed, you will not find it. At the outset, you must understand that the very nature of God is different than anything you might conceive and that you yourself are not who or what you might think you are.

God will forever be a mystery, the nameless and unknown. God is completely other than what we might think. Discovering this is a troubling thing, shaking one to the core! To draw near to the Lord is a deeply troubling thing, for I must become no-thing, empty of myself, that the Lord might enter and the Holy Spirit fill me. God is No-thing and I must become no-thing to enter into union with the Holy One of Being If you think you are something, if you think you are a substantial and independent self-existence, a solid or fixed entity, it is greatly troubling to discover that your secret center is no-thing, that you are empty of any substantial or independent self-existence.

There is another sort of troubling that may come with the dawn of higher awareness and drawing near to the Lord. In the Sacred Unity that God is, you encounter absolute and ultimate perfection, the primordial emptiness that is at one and the same time Divine fullness. Before the perfection of the Lord, your own imperfection is glaring and stark in contrast, a profoundly troubling thing to discover and, indeed, painful. Drawing nearer to the Lord, you discover how very far away from God you are. This is the cause of the dark night of the soul of which the mystics speak in their journey.

LOGION 3

Jesus said, "If those who lead you say to you, 'See, the kingdom is in the sky,' then the birds of the air will precede you. If they say to you, 'It is in the sea,' then the fish will precede you. Rather, the kingdom is inside of you, and it is outside of you. When you come to know yourselves, then you will become known, and you will realize that it is you who are the sons of the living father. But if you will not know yourselves, you dwell in poverty and it is you who are that poverty."

The kingdom of heaven, is within you and all around you— yet, if you do not know that the kingdom is within you, then you will not see the kingdom outside of you. Such is the nature of reality, this magical display of consciousness. The inside and the outside are not separate but are intimately connected. The reality of your experience is the magical display of your own consciousness. A change in consciousness brings about a corresponding change in the reality you encounter. A change in the reality you encounter is an expression of a change in consciousness.

Augustine, however, sensed the obstruction of such dualistic language when he said: "There are many people who claim to be inside the Church, but they are really outside it, for they do not practice the love and the life of Christ; and there are many who are apparently outside the Church, but who are really inside it, for they do practice the love and life of Christ."

Whether heaven or hell, it is all a state of mind, a condition of consciousness-being. The kingdom of heaven is not a place, but a spaciousness in consciousness, just as hell is a severe confinement and limitation upon consciousness.

So many souls are asleep and dreaming strange and fitful dreams. They are asleep and do not know that they are dreaming and so cannot awaken in the dream to transform it. To the awakened ones, the holy ones, it is a sad and sorry sight . It is a vision of sorrow to behold the nightmares created by self-grasping, desire, and fear, and all of the suffering that naturally follows. The awakened ones know the world of Supernal Light here and now, yet they also know how very real the suffering is of those who remain ignorant and asleep.

What is to be attained? Knowing and experiencing yourself as part of the Sacred Unity that is God, here and now. You have always been part of that Sacred Unity, are and always will be part of that Sacred Unity, the Holy One of Being . Never have you been separate from the Holy One. Union with God is not really an attainment; it is a present reality and truth. You need only remember the Spirit and Truth. You need only awaken and live with this awareness . It is not something you lack, but who and what you most truly are, the son or daughter of the Living God— the child of the Light, the Light of awareness itself.

So we see that to work for the coming of the Kingdom implies a twofold movement: toward the inwardness of all things, spiritualizing matter; and toward the outwardness of things, manifesting the Spirit, incarnating it fully within the space, time, society, and situations that are ours.

LOGION 7

Yeshua said: Fortunate is the lion eaten by a human, for lion becomes human. Unfortunate is the human eaten by a lion, for human becomes lion.

Some would interpret this lion, which a human may eat but which must not eat a human, as a symbol of the libido, the life force within us. "Eating" the libido means taming and mastering it so that it becomes humanized and ultimately transformed into a force of love. On the other hand, when we are "eaten"—that is, manipulated—by it, we are conditioned by this libido and become its slave. In gnostic thought, the lion is more the ego or mental activity that stalks us, devouring our attention and our true identity, which is the Self.

Fortunate is the "little me" integrated into the Self, for it has found its true place. Unfortunate is the person so devoured by ego (that "bundle of memories," as Krishnamurti called it) that he forgets the Self. Then human becomes lion (egocentric): the ego-persona co-opts and devours everything in sight.

LOGION 10

Jesus said, "I have cast fire upon the world, and see, I am guarding it until it blazes."

In the Gospel of Luke, Yeshua expresses his impatience to see the fire lit. But in the Gospel of Thomas it would seem that he is preserving the fire.

The Master comes with a holy fire, a fire-consuming fire, making all like unto itself, Divine. The Master imparts the fire, kindles the fire, and tends the holy fire until it blazes and transforms the disciple. The disciple, too, once receiving the holy fire, must kindle and tend it until it blazes, the Master and disciple acting together so that initiation comes to fruition.

There is a holy continuum adepts or masters tend that empowers the continuum of spiritual practice and spiritual living among their disciples and at the same time blesses and protects those they have received as disciples. Once such a connection is actually formed, it remains until it is brought to fruition or completion, the actual completion occurring when the disciple imparts the initiation to another person. Here, the Master speaks of this secret continuum. In this way, passing from one to another, the whole world is set on fire with the Word of the Lord. The Master is also speaking of something more, for Yeshua Messiah is an incarnation of the great World Teacher. More than a prophet, he is Messiah, and he brings into the world a new Divine consciousness-force along with a new dimension of teachings and initiations corresponding to this Supernal Light-force.

Embodying this Divine consciousness-force, he transmits it to his immediate disciples and, through his disciples, to the larger collective of humanity and the world, initiating a Light-transmission that passes from one generation to another through the succession of apostles, the initiates who hold the secret keys of the mysteries that the Master taught and who embody something of the Light-force he brought into the world.

LOGION 16

Jesus said, "Men think, perhaps, that it is peace which I have come to cast upon the world. They do not know that it is dissension which I have come to cast upon the earth: fire, sword, and war. For there will be five in a house: three will be against two, and two against three, the father against the son, and the son against the father. And they will stand solitary."

The Peace that Christ offers us is neither euphoria nor some kind of tranquilizer. It is the essential Peace of Being, which does not depend upon favorable outer circumstances. In order to discover this Peace, which nothing and no one can take from us, it is necessary to be willing to undergo the fire, the sword, and war—in other words, to experience the purification, the discrimination that can shake us out of our false sense of security.

When Yeshua says that he comes to bring us fire, sword, and conflict, he is also offering us the tools of our own liberation. He is teaching us how to break free of the false identifications or self-images to which we are so attached, but that prevent us from attaining our naked reality, free of illusions. Whoever has been through liberating trials is able to stand, alone and simplified—here, we have used two words for one word that is difficult to translate: monakhos, which is often poorly translated as "monk." Monakhos does not necessarily imply celibacy; it refers to those who move toward the One (monos), toward the integration of all their aspects—body, soul, and spirit—so as to become "monogenetic," like the Son, one entire river flowing toward the Father.

This solitude is not a separation from others. On the contrary, it allows a deeper meeting with others, meeting them in their own essential solitude.

LOGION 17

Jesus said, "I shall give you what no eye has seen and what no ear has heard and what no hand has touched and what has never occurred to the human mind."

What Yeshua offers here is not something that can be thought, felt, seen, or imagined. Thus he affirms the transcendence of uncreated Being. To say "I know God" can be only presumption and falsehood. While making himself known, God still remains unknowable. Here, the Gospel of Thomas shows itself as the source of traditions such as Hesychasm, which simultaneously affirm the inaccessible character of God and the reality of participation in his Being. From this, Gregory Palamas, the fourteenth-century Greek

Orthodox saint, made the distinction between energy and essence. We can never experience the core of the sun, yet we can warm ourselves in its rays. This is also the paradox of union with the divine: It is neither fusion nor separation.

LOGION 18

The disciples said to Jesus, "Tell us how our end will be."

Jesus said, "Have you discovered, then, the beginning, that

you look for the end? For where the beginning is, there will

the end be. Blessed is he who will take his place in the

beginning; he will know the end and will not experience

death."

Every present moment, in its greatest depths, reveals the

alpha and the omega. Instead of asking questions about the

end, we would do better to attend to the ever-present

Source, where all life, thought, movement, and being are

born.

LOGION 19

Jesus said, "Blessed is he who came into being before he came into being. If you become my disciples and listen to my words, these stones will minister to you. (For there are five trees for you in Paradise which remain undisturbed summer and winter and whose leaves do not fall. Whoever becomes acquainted with them will not experience death.")

We can also relate this logion to the famous statement of Yeshua for which it is said he was crucified: "Before Abraham was, I Am." This means that before entering into the space-time continuum, which includes the historical Abraham, before any existence, I Am. And this evokes the Divine Name, the Uncreated. Meister Eckhart paraphrases this word of Yeshua: "Before I was born, I Am, for all eternity." Blessed are those who, while still in space-time, become conscious of their Being in eternity, for they are in this world but not of it, and even stones will serve them.

LOGION 21

(21) (Mary said to Jesus, "Whom are your disciples like?" He said, "They are like children who have settled in a field which is not theirs. When the owners of the field come, they will say, 'Let us have back our field.' They (will) undress in their presence in order to let them have back their field and to give it back to them. Therefore I say, if the owner of a house knows that the thief is coming, he will begin his vigil before he comes and will not let him dig through into his house of his domain to carry away his goods.) You, then, be on your guard against the world. Arm yourselves with great strength lest the robbers find a

way to come to you, for the difficulty which you expect will (surely) materialize. Let there be among you a man of understanding. When the grain ripened, he came quickly with his sickle in his hand and reaped it. Whoever has ears to hear, let him hear."

The gnostic initiate does not wait upon the Second Coming of Christ, continuing to live in ignorance. In faith, the initiate seeks knowledge of Christ within , labors actively to bring the Christ-self forward, and lives according to that Truth and Light revealed. To gnostic initiates, the attainment, the image of the Lord, is the path. Practicing and living the attainment, they bring forth the fruit of the attainment and so embody something of the Christ-Spirit.

are. Spiritual practice is remembering and awakening and so setting yourself free. The disciple is one who is awakening, just as the master is one who is awake.

Resurrection is not an attainment in death but rather an attainment in life. Therefore, even before the enactment of the mystery of crucifixion and resurrection, our Lord and Savior could proclaim , "I am the resurrection and life." Who is the thief that would steal the Divine Life from you? It is ignorance and forgetfulness and the cosmic forces that support the Darkness that has dominion over this world. While in this world, you must be on your guard and not be distracted, lest you fall asleep, lose yourself in forgetfulness again, and so fail to awaken and set yourself free.

LOGION 22

(Jesus saw infants being suckled. He said to his disciples, "These infants being suckled are like those who enter the kingdom."

They said to him, "Shall we then, as children, enter the kingdom?"

Jesus said to them), "When you make the two one, and when you make the inside like the outside and the outside like the inside, and the above like the below, (and when you make the male and the female one and the same, so that the male not be male nor the female female; and when you fashion eyes in the place of an eye, and a hand in place of a hand, and a foot in place of a foot, and a likeness in place of a likeness;) then will you enter the kingdom."

The disciples conclude that to become like an infant is sufficient in order to enter into the Kingdom. But Yeshua reminds them that the infant is also a symbol of nonduality, and that it is delusive to attempt literally to be like a child, harboring childish behavior or attitudes in ourselves.

Rather, we should work to integrate all the dimensions of our being.

LOGION 28

Jesus said, "I took my place in the midst of the world, and I appeared to them in flesh. I found all of them intoxicated; I found none of them thirsty. And my soul became afflicted for the sons of men, because they are blind in their hearts and do not have sight; for empty they came into the world, and empty too they seek to leave the world. But for the moment they are intoxicated. When they shake off their wine, then they will repent."

The word "intoxication," used by the Master, is a perfect analogy. In fact, it is quite wonderful, for he tells you that this ignorance and forgetfulness and the suffering that follows is not a permanent state. Rather, any time you are ready and willing to stop consuming the intoxicant, you can sober up and regain your intelligence and lucidity. He goes further, saying that eventually every soul will shake off the intoxicant and repent— that is to say, every soul will experience a spiritual conversion or radical change in consciousness. Not only can you sober up—eventually you will— and when you do you will experience a transformation in consciousness! In the midst of great horror and darkness, the Lord offers hope! Before you can seek sobriety, you must recognize that you are drunk and the negative affect/ effect of the intoxication. You must see the sorrow and suffering drunkenness causes and how you become someone or something other than your true self. You must look and see clearly where selfishness, desire, and fear carry you, and realize the unhappiness and unhealthiness caused by it. Until a drunk is able to admit to being a drunk and able to see how it ruins one's life, he or she will not, actually cannot, attain sobriety. The same is true in terms of the intoxication of ignorance and darkness. Therefore, quite naturally, "confession of ignorance and sin" precedes the holy baptism.

LOGION 29

Jesus said, "If the flesh came into being because of spirit, it is a wonder. But if spirit came into being because of the body, it is a wonder of wonders. Indeed, I am amazed at how this great wealth has made its home in this poverty."

To allow holy awe and wonder to emerge is to experience, to some degree, something of the presence of God in that very moment. The greater the intensity of awe and wonder, the more one enters and is entered by the living presence.

Life and Nature herself is a gate into the Divine presence through which you may pass any time you wish— all you must do is allow yourself to be amazed.

To speak of faith in God is something more than merely believing in the existence of God.

Rather, it is belief with understanding in the ever-more you can be in the Spirit of God, the ever-becoming of yourself and the whole of creation. It is faith and hope in the infinite and exhaustless Divine potential.

LOGION 38

Jesus said, "Many times have you desired to hear these words which I am saying to you, and you have no one else to hear them from. There will be days when you will look for me and will not find me."

According to the Manichean Psalms, the Savior transmitted this logion so that the eleven disciples would recognize later that it was the Christ who was calling them. Mary Magdalene would also evoke these words from Yeshua: "Remember what I revealed of myself to you on the Mount of Olives: I have something to say, and no one to say it to." The logion continues, with Yeshua speaking of the day when they will seek but not find him. But why seek the Christ, the Living One, among the dead? The right moment is now. Every day is the day of salvation and every instant the time of Encounter.

LOGION 39

Jesus said, "The pharisees and the scribes have taken the keys of knowledge (gnosis) and hidden them. They themselves have not entered, nor have they allowed to enter those who wish to. You, however, be as wise as serpents and as innocent as doves."

The knowledge communicated by sacred texts is one of attention and simplicity, as indicated by the following words of this logion: "[B]e as alert as the serpent and as simple as the dove." A gnostic is not a person with any special knowledge, but rather a simple human being with a clear and open heart and no self-concern or self-importance, someone who is attentive to what is in front of him or her. The gnosis taught by Yeshua is one that develops a meditative attitude toward what is, an attitude that is nondualist, nonrationalizing, and free of projection and judgment. Gnosis is simply seeing things as they are.

There is a remarkable beauty in Yeshua's image of serpent

and dove. The serpent crawls upon the earth while the

dove flies in the sky. Thus we are told to ground ourselves

on earth without losing touch with our thrust upward into

the skies. To hold both these animal qualities is to realize

the union of opposites, of earth and heaven.

LOGION 42

Jesus said, "Become passers-by."

One who knows him- or herself a traveler, passing through

the world and the experience of this life, cannot be bound

by the dominion of cosmic forces that rules over this world

when the time comes to pass out of the world. Knowing

oneself as a traveler, a soul of Light coming from the

source of Light and Life, one is free to ascend and pass beyond. Yet anyone attached to this world, and the name and form assumed in this life, is not free to pass beyond.

To be a passerby is also to be moving toward the other shore, from the shadows to the light, from this world to the Father, as Yeshua taught—to move from what is always passing to what does not pass, to awaken to the life beyond birth and death, resurrected upon the other shore of ourselves. People said of St. Bernard that he had a very alert look, the appearance of someone who is constantly traveling, as if always on a pilgrimage to Jerusalem. Passersby see all things for the first and last time. They never look back and they savor each instant as the very place of passage of the Eternal Now.

LOGION 50

Jesus said, "If they say to you, 'Where did you come from?', say to them, 'We came from the light, the place where the light came into being on its own accord and established itself and became manifest through their image.' (If they say to you, 'Is it you?', say, 'We are its children, we are the elect of the living father.' If they ask you, 'What is the sign of your father in you?', say to them, 'It is movement and repose.'")

The ancient triple question "Where do I come from? Where am I going? Who am I?" finds an unequivocal response in this logion. You come from the Light, you are going toward the Light, you are the Light. This is the reality of the Living Son in us, who abides in the very heart of changing appearances. The sign of our link with this luminous Reality is "movement and . . . repose." This is a union of opposites, the resolution of the seeming

contradiction between action and contemplation: calmness

within action and vitality within repose.

LOGION 58

Jesus said, "Blessed is the man who has suffered and found

life."

If you must endure sorrow and suffering, then let it not be

without purpose and meaning. Seek to draw from it the

blessings that may be found in it, so that, when the period

of sorrow or suffering has passed, you will have the good

from it. When you meet the challenges of life in this way,

you will naturally be blessed and your faith will grow

stronger and your soul more refined. You will find Life! St.

James has written, "Whenever you face trials of any kind,

consider it joy, because you know that the testing of your

faith produces endurance; and let your endurance have its

full effect, so that you may be mature and complete, lacking

in nothing." Yes, indeed! Be joyful in the face of trials and

tribulations and sorrow and suffering will be transformed!

When met in this way, every challenge of life is an

opportunity for growth and development of the soul and

spiritual evolution toward Christ-consciousness.

When you open your heart, making room for everyone and

everything and for the Lord, suffering is decreased and

passes more swiftly. This is simple wisdom of life

experience.

LOGION 59

Jesus said, "Take heed of the living one while you are alive, lest you die and seek to see him and be unable to do so."

What more need be said?

LOGION 61

(Jesus said, "Two will rest on a bed: the one will die, and the other will live."

Salome said, "Who are you, man, that you ... have come up on my couch and eaten from my table?")

Jesus said to her, "I am he who exists from the undivided. (I was given some of the things of my father.")

I come from the One who is Openness. Rilke once said that Openness is the least blasphemous name for God. It is the name that is the least defining and qualifying. Openness is the infinite Space within the very heart of space, containing all and contained by nothing.

The whole process of human transformation is one of opening on all levels: the physical (release of stress), the psychic (unraveling the knots of memory), and the spiritual (allowing love, light, and forgiveness to live and radiate in us). The goal of this transformation is to dwell in Openness, where the body is open to the energies of the cosmos, the heart is open to a deep compassion, and the mind is as clear as a mirror, serenely reflecting the multitude of appearances. A totally open human being is not formless, but is instead capable of allowing the One to manifest. The Unity of all things then becomes manifest in and through that human form. As long as there is any fear, constriction, closure, division of the heart, or dualism, the light cannot enter. We can close the shutters on all the windows of the house, which is so much the worse for the air inside, yet the sun goes on shining.

LOGION 65

(He said, "There was a good man who owned a vineyard. He leased it to tenant farmers so that they might work it and he might collect the produce from them. He sent his servant so that the tenants might give him the produce of the vineyard. They seized his servant and beat him, all but killing him. The servant went back and told his master. The master said, 'Perhaps he did not recognize them.' He sent another servant. The tenants beat this one as well.) Then the owner sent his son and said, 'Perhaps they will show respect to my son.' Because the tenants knew that it was he who was the heir to the vineyard, they seized him and killed him. Let him who has ears hear."

The standard interpretation of this well-known parable is that God has planted his "vine" in this world in the form of his servants, the sages and prophets, but people refuse to respect them or listen to their message. But in addition to his servants, he sends his son, a holy one who incarnates the Presence, Image, and Likeness of the Father in the heart of this space-time. The drama of the killing of the son is the killing of the Christ in ourselves. It is the same madness, the same murder: stifling the likeness of God, or Love, in ourselves.

LOGION 68

Jesus said, "Blessed are you when you are hated and persecuted. Wherever you have been persecuted they will find no place."

In every human being there is a place that hatred and persecution can never reach: the Self, the uncreated Being beyond the identification of "I" as suffering victim. This is the space of inalienable freedom that empowers us to say, with Christ, "My life cannot be taken, for I have already given it"—or the famous words: "Forgive them, for they know not what they do." Blame and persecution may even be considered beatitudes, inasmuch as they awaken in us an authentic Love for our enemies, putting us in touch with that freedom which no circumstance can ever affect.

LOGION 69

Jesus said, "Blessed are they who have been persecuted within themselves. It is they who have truly come to know the father.

He is speaking of an inward conscious struggle for growth and refinement of oneself on moral and spiritual levels— an evolution of the psychic and spiritual dimensions of oneself according to the Truth and Light revealed in one's own experience. During periods of our early development on the path, our conscience is very likely to persecute us, convicting us of our ignorance and missing the mark, so that we are not satisfied to remain in Darkness, but are compelled to seek the Light. The persecution of which the Master is speaking is akin to the dark nights of the soul, of which St. John of the Cross wrote. Only those willing to pass through ordeals of spiritual growth and advancement will come to a full and conscious unity with the Lord and know the most intimate communion in the Spirit of the Lord.

LOGION 77

(Jesus said, "It is I who am the light which is above them all. It is I who am the all. From me did the all come forth, and unto me did the all extend.) Split a piece of wood, and I am there. Lift up the stone, and you will find me there."

When Yeshua says "I am the All," he refers to the fact that he manifests in himself the integration of all polarities and opposites. He incarnates the union of the human and the divine, the finite and the infinite, time and eternity.

For a disciple of Jesus, work is not a danger, a burden, nor a hardship, but the very presence of the Lord! "You will find me when you break up stones, and I am there while you split the wood." In Matthew 18:20 Jesus promises to come to those who pray in his name; here, he promises to come to those who do hard work in his name. In contrast to this, a metaphysical interpretation of the logion is that all things participate in the very essence of Being, according to their mode and degree.

LOGION 82

Jesus said, "He who is near me is near the fire, and he who is far from me is far from the kingdom."

To pass through the holy gate of the kingdom of heaven, you cannot be lukewarm, but must be hot, on fire with the indwelling Spirit, filled with divine passion. No one knows the presence of the Lord and the Lord himself who is not passionate for the holy Shekinah as he himself was passionate. Such holy passion burns oneself utterly away and there is only the Beloved. At the same time, holy passion itself is transforming and illuminating and is, itself, the Divine Life, for what passion comes is the passion of the inner self or Christ-self, a new and Divine consciousness and being filled with Light and Life.

LOGION 89

Jesus said, "Why do you wash the outside of the cup? Do you not realize that he who made the inside is the same one who made the outside?"

A radical change in consciousness is necessary to enter into Christ-consciousness. In truth, Christ-consciousness is something more than a change of mental concepts and emotions and the like. It is a transcendence of the mental and vital being altogether; the transformation of the mental, vital, and even physical consciousness through the Divine power that comes with self-realization in Christ. One must actually be reborn and transfigured by the supernal force that comes from above.

This is yet another way in which Yeshua invites us to realize the non-duality of Being and appearance, inner and outer. To abandon duplicity and hypocrisy is to rediscover transparency. It is also to discover that the same One is both inside and outside. The space inside the cup is the same space that contains the Universe. One moment of true silence, and we are in the heart of that Silence from which all creative words arise.

LOGION 92

Jesus said, "Seek and you will find. Yet, what you asked me about in former times and which I did not tell you then, now I do desire to tell, but you do not inquire after it."

Asking is receiving, seeking is finding, knocking is the opening of the door that you might enter.

The mystical journey and spiritual life is, by nature, a sacred quest to which there is no final answer. Rather, it is a continuum of self-expression and experience through which the soul advances and evolves consciously. It is an on-going gradual and organic process of exploration and penetration of the holy mysteries of God and Creation ,

and thus the unfoldment of one's own self-realization.

Those who seek will discover, and continuing to seek

beyond discovery, God will continue to reveal Godself

without end, for God is Ain Sof, the One-Without-End,

the infinite and eternal. This continual self-revelation of

God and communion in God is the reward of the righteous

and elect, a reward inherent in living the Divine Life.

LOGION 93

Jesus said: "Do not give what is holy to dogs, lest they

throw them on the dung-heap. Do not throw the pearls to

swine…"

Here, the Master makes it clear that the esoteric wisdom,

the inner and secret teachings, are not for everyone. While

outer teachings may be more freely shared, the inner and secret level of the teachings must be shared only under the guidance of the Holy Spirit with those who are ready to receive them and who will not profane them. We are charged to share and give what we have received, for only in this way is our reception fulfilled, but we must impart the transmission consciously, with discernment and with skillful methods, giving to each person what the Spirit would have us give and what is good for them.

Receiving, we are called to share and give of ourselves and what we have received, that the Light might be in extension and others might also receive and so be joined to the mystical body of Christ. We do not seek to receive for ourselves alone, but in order to be empowered and have something to share and give to others. Our aim as initiates in the Christ-Spirit is to be channels of God's Grace, vehicles of his continual outpouring of blessings. Yet in the process of sharing and giving of ourselves and what we have received, we must be alert and act with awareness, seeking the guidance of the Holy Spirit regarding God's Will.

LOGION 103

Jesus said, "Fortunate is the man who knows where the brigands will enter, so that he may get up, muster his domain, and arm himself before they invade."

First, we may understand the Master as speaking of the virtue and necessity of self-knowledge, which among other things includes the knowledge of personal strength and weakness. Knowing areas of personal weakness, we can then work on those aspects of ourselves to overcome whatever weakness , impurity , or imperfection may be present. We can work to strengthen what is weak, purify what is impure, and work out the imperfections we find. In order to consciously evolve, we must acquire self - knowledge through the agency of the silent witness, being awake and alert in our daily living, for only with self-knowledge can we work with the Holy Spirit to refine and shape ourselves in the image of Christ.

To stay awake is to be centered, to gather strength and not waste it. This is a condition for maintaining calm and confidence during times of trial, when the thieves, the enemies of Life, come to rob our energies. We may also know the time of the thieves' arrival. Once more, this refers to self-knowledge: knowing our own tendencies toward weakness or depression without judging ourselves.

LOGION 108

Jesus said, "He who will drink from my mouth will become like me. I myself shall become he, and the things that are hidden will be revealed to him."

Our goal is not just to follow the Christ, but to allow ourselves to be filled with his substance, informed by his Word, and to become him. We must trace back John's words to the very Breath of the mouth of Christ. Jewish tradition says that Moses died from a kiss of God. The butterfly flew into the burning bush and became fire.

To drink from the mouth of the Anointed One implies two things. First, a very deep intimacy, as though the intimacy of a lover to their beloved; and second, an active living and experiencing of the teachings given— hence , living the

Word of the Lord. These two things are, in fact , one and the same, for the lover of the Lord will draw near unto the Lord by living his teachings and practicing righteousness, thus becoming more and more like unto the Anointed One. The natural result and climax of such nearness or likeness is that the Anointed One manifests as you. To live the teachings of Christ is to become Christ-like and, yet more, to embody Christ, the Spirit of Christ manifesting through your person. This is the aim of the Mystic Christian initiate. The things that are hidden are revealed as one enters ever more deeply into the mystical experience of Christ; this is an obvious truth. Many things can only be revealed through direct spiritual experience. Except within the context of the experience itself (such as with another person sharing the same experience), these things cannot be communicated. Thus, experience is the basis of initiation. Here, the Master is speaking of the inmost secret initiations that transpire through direct experience of Messianic or supernal consciousness. This emphasis upon direct personal spiritual experience is the foundation of Mystical Christianity. By "Mystical" is meant knowledge acquired through personal and direct spiritual experience. Because of this emphasis, central to the teachings of Mystical Christianity are methods of spiritual practice, mystical prayer, and prophetic meditation, through which the aspirant may attain some degree of direct experience and so bring their faith to fruit in gnosis of the Christ-Spirit.

LOGION 113

His disciples said to him, "When will the kingdom come?" Jesus said: "It will not come by waiting for it. It will not be a matter of saying 'here it is' or 'there it is.' Rather, the kingdom of the father is spread out upon the earth, and men do not see it."

Human society or the world directly reflect the state of consciousness of the individuals forming the collective . The world that we experience is the radiance of our own consciousness or is created by our state of consciousness. In truth, the reality we experience and our state of consciousness are completely interconnected. Therefore, to change the reality of our experience, we need to bring about a corresponding change in our consciousness. Mystical attainment means a conscious unification with God; which brings about a corresponding change in reality or manifestation.

The Way of enlightenment is opposite to the way of unenlightened society. You must separate yourself from herd consciousness and sojourn in the opposite direction

of unenlightened society in order to realize Christ -
consciousness in yourself. Once having realized something
of a higher consciousness, you must then labor to enlighten
your society and to bring about a greater good.

The true nature of the Second Coming is a dawn of Christ-
consciousness in a sufficient number of individuals to
effect a radical transformation.

To accomplish this sacred duty, we must engage with the
teaching of the first logion of the Gospel of Thomas and
ask ourselves if we are truly living the interpretation of
these words in our body, heart, and mind. Only then can
the creative words of the Living Yeshua give rise to the
new Person in us, in the image and likeness of the Eternal
Son.

3

Additional Sayings

What will death mean to that one who experiences

Messianic consciousness and dwells in the kingdom of God

while in this life? Indeed, death will not mean what it

means to the ordinary person, for that one is not so self-

identified with mortal name and form, but knows oneself

as an immortal Spirit, a bornless and therefore deathless

Spirit. Likewise, this person knows that the kingdom of

heaven is present within and all around, always— that upon

death one's experience of Christ will continue in a more

subtle and sublime form, having shed the physical body.

With this knowledge, death is no longer death and the

adversary has no power over the soul, whether in this

world or in the world to come. Such a person is awakened

and therefore free, having a continuity of awareness

throughout all states of existence . Death will come, as it

has for all prophets and saints, but it will just be an

appearance of departure— a transition to another mode of

existence, no more or less real than falling asleep, only to

dream and awaken again. Death, for the Gnostic, is not an

end as much as a new beginning. Ultimately, death has no

substantial reality, but is merely a natural moment of

transition. Knowing this changes everything.

(8) And he said, "The man is like a wise fisherman who cast his net into the sea and drew it up from the sea full of small fish. Among them the wise fisherman found a fine large fish. He threw all the small fish back into the sea and chose the large fish without difficulty. Whoever has ears to hear, let him hear."

(9) Jesus said, "Now the sower went out, took a handful (of seeds), and scattered them. Some fell on the road; the birds came and gathered them up. Others fell on the rock, did not take root in the soil, and did not produce ears. And others fell on thorns; they choked the seed(s) and worms ate them. And others fell on the good soil and it produced good fruit: it bore sixty per measure and a hundred and twenty per measure."

(11) Jesus said, "This heaven will pass away, and the one above it will pass away. The dead are not alive, and the living will not die. In the days when you consumed what is dead, you made it what is alive. When you come to dwell in the light, what will you do? On the day when you were one you became two. But when you become two, what will you do?"

(12) The disciples said to Jesus, "We know that you will depart from us. Who is to be our leader?"
Jesus said to them, "Wherever you are, you are to go to James the righteous, for whose sake heaven and earth came into being."

(13) Jesus said to his disciples, "Compare me to someone and tell me whom I am like."
Simon Peter said to him, "You are like a righteous angel."
Matthew said to him, "You are like a wise philosopher."

Thomas said to him, "Master, my mouth is wholly incapable of saying whom you are like."

Jesus said, "I am not your master. Because you have drunk, you have become intoxicated from the bubbling spring which I have measured out."

And he took him and withdrew and told him three things. When Thomas returned to his companions, they asked him, "What did Jesus say to you?"

Thomas said to them, "If I tell you one of the things which he told me, you will pick up stones and throw them at me; a fire will come out of the stones and burn you up."

(14) Jesus said to them, "If you fast, you will give rise to sin for yourselves; and if you pray, you will be condemned; and if you give alms, you will do harm to your spirits. When you go into any land and walk about in the districts, if they receive you, eat what they will set before you, and heal the

sick among them. For what goes into your mouth will not defile you, but that which issues from your mouth - it is that which will defile you."

(15) Jesus said, "When you see one who was not born of woman, prostrate yourselves on your faces and worship him. That one is your father."

(20) The disciples said to Jesus, "Tell us what the kingdom of heaven is like."
He said to them, "It is like a mustard seed. It is the smallest of all seeds. But when it falls on tilled soil, it produces a great plant and becomes a shelter for birds of the sky."

(23) Jesus said, "I shall choose you, one out of a thousand, and two out of ten thousand, and they shall stand as a single one."

(24) His disciples said to him, "Show us the place where you are, since it is necessary for us to seek it."

He said to them, "Whoever has ears, let him hear. There is light within a man of light, and he lights up the whole world. If he does not shine, he is darkness."

(26) Jesus said, "You see the mote in your brother's eye, but you do not see the beam in your own eye. When you cast the beam out of your own eye, then you will see clearly to cast the mote from your brother's eye."

(27) <Jesus said,> "If you do not fast as regards the world, you will not find the kingdom. If you do not observe the Sabbath as a Sabbath, you will not see the father."

(30) Jesus said, "Where there are three gods, they are gods. Where there are two or one, I am with him."

(31) Jesus said, "No prophet is accepted in his own village; no physician heals those who know him."

(32) Jesus said, "A city being built on a high mountain and fortified cannot fall, nor can it be hidden."

(33) Jesus said, "Preach from your housetops that which you will hear in your ear. For no one lights a lamp and puts it under a bushel, nor does he put it in a hidden place, but rather he sets it on a lampstand so that everyone who enters and leaves will see its light."

(34) Jesus said, "If a blind man leads a blind man, they will both fall into a pit."

(35) Jesus said, "It is not possible for anyone to enter the house of a strong man and take it by force unless he binds his hands; then he will (be able to) ransack his house."

(36) Jesus said, "Do not be concerned from morning until evening and from evening until morning about what you will wear."

(37) His disciples said, "When will you become revealed to us and when shall we see you?"

Jesus said, "When you disrobe without being ashamed and take up your garments and place them under your feet like little children and tread on them, then will you see the son of the living one, and you will not be afraid"

(40) Jesus said, "A grapevine has been planted outside of the father, but being unsound, it will be pulled up by its roots and destroyed."

(41) Jesus said, "Whoever has something in his hand will receive more, and whoever has nothing will be deprived of even the little he has."

(43) His disciples said to him, "Who are you, that you should say these things to us?"

<Jesus said to them,> "You do not realize who I am from what I say to you, but you have become like the Jews, for they (either) love the tree and hate its fruit (or) love the fruit and hate the tree."

(44) Jesus said, "Whoever blasphemes against the father will be forgiven, and whoever blasphemes against the son will be forgiven, but whoever blasphemes against the holy spirit will not be forgiven either on earth or in heaven."

(45) Jesus said, "Grapes are not harvested from thorns, nor are figs gathered from thistles, for they do not produce fruit. A good man brings forth good from his storehouse; an evil man brings forth evil things from his evil

storehouse, which is in his heart, and says evil things. For out of the abundance of the heart he brings forth evil things."

(46) Jesus said, "Among those born of women, from Adam until John the Baptist, there is no one so superior to John the Baptist that his eyes should not be lowered (before him). Yet I have said, whichever one of you comes to be a child will be acquainted with the kingdom and will become superior to John."

(47) Jesus said, "It is impossible for a man to mount two horses or to stretch two bows. And it is impossible for a servant to serve two masters; otherwise, he will honor the one and treat the other contemptuously. No man drinks old wine and immediately desires to drink new wine. And new wine is not put into old wineskins, lest they burst; nor is old wine put into a new wineskin, lest it spoil it. An old

patch is not sewn onto a new garment, because a tear would result."

(48) Jesus said, "If two make peace with each other in this one house, they will say to the mountain, 'Move Away,' and it will move away."

(49) Jesus said, "Blessed are the solitary and elect, for you will find the kingdom. For you are from it, and to it you will return."

(51) His disciples said to him, "When will the repose of the dead come about, and when will the new world come?" He said to them, "What you look forward to has already come, but you do not recognize it."

(52) His disciples said to him, "Twenty-four prophets spoke in Israel, and all of them spoke in you."

He said to them, "You have omitted the one living in your presence and have spoken (only) of the dead."

(53) His disciples said to him, "Is circumcision beneficial or not?"

He said to them, "If it were beneficial, their father would beget them already circumcised from their mother. Rather, the true circumcision in spirit has become completely profitable."

(54) Jesus said, "Blessed are the poor, for yours is the kingdom of heaven."

(55) Jesus said, "Whoever does not hate his father and his mother cannot become a disciple to me. And whoever does not hate his brothers and sisters and take up his cross in my way will not be worthy of me."

(56) Jesus said, "Whoever has come to understand the world has found (only) a corpse, and whoever has found a corpse is superior to the world."

(57) Jesus said, "The kingdom of the father is like a man who had good seed. His enemy came by night and sowed weeds among the good seed. The man did not allow them to pull up the weeds; he said to them, 'I am afraid that you will go intending to pull up the weeds and pull up the wheat along with them.' For on the day of the harvest the weeds will be plainly visible, and they will be pulled up and burned."

(60) <They saw> a Samaritan carrying a lamb on his way to Judea. He said to his disciples, "That man is round about the lamb."

They said to him, "So that he may kill it and eat it."

He said to them, "While it is alive, he will not eat it, but

only when he has killed it and it has become a corpse."

They said to him, "He cannot do so otherwise."

He said to them, "You too, look for a place for yourself

within repose, lest you become a corpse and be eaten."

<...> "I am your disciple."

<...> "Therefore I say, if he is destroyed, he will be filled

with light, but if he is divided, he will be filled with

darkness."

(62) Jesus said, "It is to those who are worthy of my

mysteries that I tell my mysteries. Do not let your left

(hand) know what your right (hand) is doing."

(64) Jesus said, "A man had received visitors. And when he

had prepared the dinner, he sent his servant to invite the

guests.

He went to the first one and said to him, 'My master invites you.' He said, 'I have claims against some merchants. They are coming to me this evening. I must go and give them my orders. I ask to be excused from the dinner.'

He went to another and said to him, 'My master has invited you.' He said to him, 'I have just bought a house and am required for the day. I shall not have any spare time.'

He went to another and said to him, 'My master invites you.' He said to him, 'My friend is going to get married, and I am to prepare the banquet. I shall not be able to come. I ask to be excused from the dinner.'

He went to another and said to him, 'My master invites you.' He said to him, 'I have just bought a farm, and I am on my way to collect the rent. I shall not be able to come. I ask to be excused.'

The servant returned and said to his master, 'Those whom

you invited to the dinner have asked to be excused.' The master said to his servant, 'Go outside to the streets and bring back those whom you happen to meet, so that they may dine.' Businessmen and merchants will not enter the places of my father."

Living One from offering its fruit.

(66) Jesus said, "Show me the stone which the builders have rejected. That one is the cornerstone."

(67) Jesus said, "If one who knows the all still feels a personal deficiency, he is completely deficient."

you do not have it within you."

(71) Jesus said, "I shall destroy this house, and no one will be able to build it [...]."

(72) A man said to him, "Tell my brothers to divide my father's possessions with me."

He said to him, "O man, who has made me a divider?"

He turned to his disciples and said to them, "I am not a divider, am I?"

(73) Jesus said, "The harvest is great but the laborers are few. Beseech the Lord, therefore, to send out laborers to the harvest."

(76) Jesus said, "The kingdom of the father is like a merchant who had a consignment of merchandise and who discovered a pearl. That merchant was shrewd. He sold the merchandise and bought the pearl alone for himself. You too, seek his unfailing and enduring treasure where no moth comes near to devour and no worm destroys."

(78) Jesus said, "Why have you come out into the desert? To see a reed shaken by the wind? And to see a man clothed in fine garments like your kings and your great men? Upon them are the fine garments, and they are unable to discern the truth."

(79) A woman from the crowd said to him, "Blessed are the womb which bore you and the breasts which nourished you."

He said to her, "Blessed are those who have heard the word of the father and have truly kept it. For there will be days when you will say, 'Blessed are the womb which has not conceived and the breasts which have not given milk.'"

(80) Jesus said, "He who has recognized the world has found the body, but he who has found the body is superior to the world."

(81) Jesus said, "Let him who has grown rich be king, and let him who possesses power renounce it."

(84) Jesus said, "When you see your likeness, you rejoice. But when you see your images which came into being before you, and which neither die not become manifest, how much you will have to bear!"

(85) Jesus said, "Adam came into being from a great power and a great wealth, but he did not become worthy of you. For had he been worthy, he would not have experienced death."

(86) Jesus said, "The foxes have their holes and the birds have their nests, but the son of man has no place to lay his head and rest."

(87) Jesus said, "Wretched is the body that is dependant upon a body, and wretched is the soul that is dependent on these two."

(88) Jesus said, "The angels and the prophets will come to you and give to you those things you (already) have. And you too, give them those things which you have, and say to yourselves, 'When will they come and take what is theirs?'"

(90) Jesus said, "Come unto me, for my yoke is easy and my lordship is mild, and you will find repose for yourselves."

(94) Jesus said, "He who seeks will find, and he who knocks will be let in."

(95) Jesus said, "If you have money, do not lend it at interest, but give it to one from whom you will not get it back."

(96) Jesus said, "The kingdom of the father is like a certain woman. She took a little leaven, concealed it in some dough, and made it into large loaves. Let him who has ears hear."

(98) Jesus said, "The kingdom of the father is like a certain man who wanted to kill a powerful man. In his own house he drew his sword and stuck it into the wall in order to find out whether his hand could carry through. Then he slew the powerful man."

(99) The disciples said to him, "Your brothers and your mother are standing outside."

He said to them, "Those here who do the will of my father are my brothers and my mother. It is they who will enter the kingdom of my father."

(100) They showed Jesus a gold coin and said to him, "Caesar's men demand taxes from us."
He said to them, "Give Caesar what belongs to Caesar, give God what belongs to God, and give me what is mine."

(102) Jesus said, "Woe to the pharisees, for they are like a dog sleeping in the manger of oxen, for neither does he eat nor does he let the oxen eat."

(104) They said to Jesus, "Come, let us pray today and let us fast."
Jesus said, "What is the sin that I have committed, or

wherein have I been defeated? But when the bridegroom leaves the bridal chamber, then let them fast and pray."

(105) Jesus said, "He who knows the father and the mother will be called the son of a harlot."

(107) Jesus said, "The kingdom is like a shepherd who had a hundred sheep. One of them, the largest, went astray. He left the ninety-nine sheep and looked for that one until he found it. When he had gone to such trouble, he said to the sheep, 'I care for you more than the ninety-nine.'"

(109) Jesus said, "The kingdom is like a man who had a hidden treasure in his field without knowing it. And after he died, he left it to his son. The son did not know (about the treasure). He inherited the field and sold it. And the one who bought it went plowing and found the treasure.

He began to lend money at interest to whomever he wished."

(110) Jesus said, "Whoever finds the world and becomes rich, let him renounce the world."

(111) Jesus said, "The heavens and the earth will be rolled up in your presence. And the one who lives from the living one will not see death." Does not Jesus say, "Whoever finds himself is superior to the world?"

(112) Jesus said, "Woe to the flesh that depends on the soul; woe to the soul that depends on the flesh."

Printed in Great Britain
by Amazon

44960827R00070